ROADS Publishing
149 Lower Baggot Street
Dublin 2
Ireland

www.roads.co

First published 2017

1

Dublin: The Considered Guide

Text copyright
© ROADS Publishing

Design and layout copyright
© ROADS Publishing

Photographs
© The copyright holders, pg. 142

Cover image
© Getty Images/David Soanes Photography

All of the businesses herein were chosen at the discretion of the publishers.
No payments or incentives were offered or received to ensure inclusion.

Art direction by
Alessio Avventuroso

Designed by
Agenzia del Contemporaneo

Printed in Italy by
Grafiche Damiani – Faenza Group SpA

978-1-909399-93-8

Dublin

The Considered Guide

Growing up, travel was a major part of my life. It was and remains an integral source of education and inspiration. When I travel, I actively search out the most interesting and innovative places. As a rule, I ask my friends and contacts in each city for a list of their favourite places. I then keep and share with others my lists of places both recommended and those I discovered myself. Therefore, I decided to create the kind of travel guide that I myself would find useful: a carefully edited selection of the best places in a city – a book that is practical, beautiful, and, crucially, trustworthy.

The Considered Guide reflects the desires of the discerning traveller who cares deeply about how they spend their valuable time and money, and who appreciates impeccable service, beautiful design and attention to detail at every price level.

I am proud to say that I visited each and every place in this guide, and can vouch for the quality of each of them as personal recommendations.

Danielle Ryan
Founder of ROADS

Introduction

Dublin City covers 115 square kilometres – a 'capital village' compared to some of its European counterparts – and is home to 1.7 million people of more than 100 nationalities. It is therefore a cosmopolitan city for its size, but has suffered severe changes in fortune over the last thirty years. During the so-called Celtic Tiger years, from the mid-1990s to the mid-2000s, Ireland – and Dublin in particular – saw a huge influx of foreign investment which hurtled the country from one of Western Europe's poorest, to one of its richest. Tech companies such as Google (and later, Facebook) made Dublin their European base, and in doing so transformed the city's Grand Canal Dock area, which remains one of the more striking new quarters within strolling distance of the city centre.

But the bubble had to burst. In September 2008 Ireland officially entered recession, and over the following years, extant problems such as unemployment, homelessness and drug abuse were exacerbated, and remain ongoing issues for the city. However, developments in the city's transport and hospital infrastructure, new business investments, and ever-strong visitor numbers are cause for optimism.

That Dublin is a city steeped in literary and historical significance is well documented. What is less widely known is how much it has developed creatively in recent years. Following the flashy but bland boom of the Celtic Tiger years, and the subsequent struggle of the recession, today it is a city on the rise, brimming with creativity.

Most of Dublin can be covered on foot, and the majority of the recommendations in this guide fall within the circle of the Royal Canal to the north and the Grand Canal to the south. Dublin is bisected by the River Liffey, reflecting a city of contrasts – Northside versus Southside, old versus new. While the Northside and Southside do have distinct personalities, misconceptions endure about both sides of the river, and a visit to Dublin would be incomplete without exploring both.

The Southside is, in general, wealthier, and houses more of the traditional tourist attractions. The Northside is historically poorer, and a centuries-long snobbery has endured that has failed to celebrate it as a thriving landscape where young creatives blend with Dublin locals whose families have lived here for generations. Thankfully, this attitude is on the wane. Capel Street is a celebrated destination for dining and nightlife, and the nearby neighbourhood of Stoneybatter is home to some of the city's best new casual eateries. The Southside, as the centre of wealth and power for hundreds of years, is where you will find exquisite Georgian architecture, museums, and wonderfully designed urban gardens. Sites of literary and political importance are everywhere, on both sides of the Liffey, and a great deal can be covered on even the shortest of visits.

Both sides also cater for the weekend visitor's food, drink and shopping requirements. Dublin is famous the world over for its vibrant nightlife, but in recent years it has seen an explosion in exciting high-quality independent restaurants and cafés that celebrate Irish ingredients in modern ways and in beautiful settings. A stand-out destination for shopping and people-watching is the city centre's Creative Quarter, which runs from South William Street to George's Street, and from Lower Stephen's Street to Exchequer Street. The nucleus of independent shops promoting Irish talent, it was designated the title in 2012 because so many exciting new design businesses, cafés, bars and restaurants had made it their home, and more continue to do so.

It is true that Dublin is one of the friendliest cities in the world, and how great it is to see this brought to bear in new artistic, cultural, and culinary endeavours. In May 2015, Ireland became the first country in the world to approve same-sex marriage by popular vote, and when thousands took to the streets to celebrate, it was clear that Dublin, while deeply proud of its one thousand years of rich and turbulent history, is a vibrant city that is looking towards a bright and inclusive future.

Locals may bemoan the absence of an underground system, but Dublin is a relatively easy city to navigate, especially as it is quite compact. If you are staying in the city centre, the vast majority of the recommendations in this guidebook can be reached on foot, but it is a good idea to purchase a Leap Visitor Card on arrival, which will allow you to get around very cheaply and quickly, and pack more into your stay. This can be bought in the airport or in the Dublin Bus office on O'Connell Street, and will set you back a reasonable €19.50 for three days' travel. This is valid on the bus, the tram and on local trains.

Getting around

From the airport
aircoach.ie

There is usually a long queue of people waiting for taxis when you arrive at the airport, but it generally moves quickly. A taxi could cost you €30 depending on where you're going, traffic, and the time of day. Dublin Bus runs a number of services into the city centre, including the 747 and 757 routes (€6 one-way). There is also the popular and quick private Aircoach service (€7 one-way into the city centre).

Dublin Bikes
dublinbikes.ie

There is an increasing number of cyclists in Dublin and, unsurprisingly, the Dublin Bikes scheme has been a huge success since it began in 2014. You simply collect a bike at a station and leave it back at any other once you have finished with it. This is a popular means of getting to work for some, so there are times when bikes are tricky to lay your hands on. There are a number of tariff options available at the stands, including a three-day rate. Check out their website for a map of the ever-increasing number of stations.

Dublin Bus
dublinbus.ie

Dublin Bus recently

introduced a City Centre Fare, costing less than €1, making crossing the city very cheap and easy. Better yet, avail of the Leap Visitor Card. Download the Dublin Bus app to find the best routes.

Luas
luas.ie

'Luas' is the Irish word for 'speed', and it's also the name of the tram system that you will see crossing the city. Major works have recently been carried out to extend the network, and to connect the two previously separate Green and Red lines. The trams are frequent and reliable, but busy during rush hours. The Red line connects the city centre with its two major train stations: Connolly and Heuston.

DART
irishrail.ie/about-us/dart-commuter

An acronym for Dublin Area Rapid Transport, the local train service is a great way to get out of the city centre for the day, especially if the weather is good. Head north for the lively seaside village of Howth, which is great for walks, ice cream, and fish and chips on a sunny day; or go south to Bray and walk alongside the cliffside as far as the lovely village of Greystones.

Hotels

The Dean

Chic, stylish and contemporary, the Dean aims to offer the experience of 'staying over at a mate's house'. Sure, if your mate's house happens to have luxury wood panelling, retro furnishings and modern Irish art decorating the walls. With fifty-two varied rooms featuring everything from bunk beds to penthouse suites, the Dean also boasts rooftop tanks which collect the Irish rainwater and reuse it. The hotel is situated in a nightlife hot spot, so even if you're not staying at the Dean, you should visit to experience Sophie's, the rooftop bar and restaurant that offers staggering views across Dublin and one of the city's best terraces.

€€€

—

33 Harcourt Street, Dublin 2
Deandublin.ie
+353 1 607 8110

The Generator

Tucked away on Smithfield Square, in the hip Dublin 7 area, the Generator is one of a series of similar hostels around the world, but each retains its own unique identity. This is especially true for the Dublin branch, which lives and breathes the local culture. Light installations made from Jameson whiskey bottles, graffiti-slashed walls and furniture made from book stacks – this hostel is as eclectic as they come. Reclaimed wooden furniture dots the open floors, and exposed brick walls give the space an industrial feel. The Generator provides traditional hostel bunk beds, but an upgrade to a premium room is worth it, and the Jacuzzi suite is ideal for a girls' weekend away.

€

—

Smithfield Square, Dublin 7
generatorhostels.com
+353 1 901 0222

Kelly's Hotel

Kelly's Hotel is located above the popular Hogan's Bar on lively South Great George's Street, a favourite haunt of Dubliners. The concept of this boutique hotel is chic urban living, which is achieved by a clean and modern design interjected with elegant period features. The rooms are crisp, airy and comfortable, free from clutter and full of light, and the executive rooms have the luxury of additional space. Breakfast is served downstairs in L'Gueuleton, a truly excellent French restaurant that should be sampled for brunch, lunch or dinner, and the hotel's adjoining No Name Bar (pg. 102) offers stylish interiors, excellent cocktails, and enjoyable views of the revellers gathering for the evening on Fade Street below.

€€

—

36 South Great George's Street, Dublin 2
kellysdublin.com
+353 1 648 0010

The Marker

The Marker Hotel opened in Dublin's Grand
Canal Dock in 2013, the cherry on the cake of a
successful regeneration project in this historic
part of the city, which is now home to tech
companies, bars, restaurants, and the Libeskind-
designed Bord Gáis Energy Theatre. The concept
of the hotel's striking chequered façade is said to
be the natural geological formations of the Burren
and the Giant's Causeway, and indeed the spa,
with its dark tile and sparkling infinity pool feels
miles from the busy city. The restaurant is very
serious about using the best of Irish produce,
and after dinner, guests can retire to the rooftop
terrace, with its breathtaking views of the city, the
sea and the Dublin Mountains.

€€€€

—

Grand Canal Square, Docklands, Dublin 2
themarkerhoteldublin.com
+353 1 687 5100

The Merrion

Oscar Wilde, W.B. Yeats and Daniel O'Connell are among
the illustrious former residents of Merrion Square. Situated
across the road from the Irish Government Buildings,
this five-star hotel might be tough on the pocket, but the
reputation is well earned. Comprised of four restored
Georgian townhouses, the interior retains much of the
grandeur and elegance of days gone by. Complemented
by antique furniture and a vast private art collection, the
hotel offers old-fashioned luxury to high-flying travellers
from around the world. With a two-star Michelin restaurant,
private gardens and a world-class spa, visitors to the
Merrion hardly need to leave after they check in.

€€€€

—

Upper Merrion Street, Dublin 2
merrionhotel.com
+353 1 603 0600

Number 31

Formerly the home of modernist architect Sam Stephenson, Number 31 is a guesthouse made up of two buildings: a classic Georgian townhouse and a cool, contemporary mews, connected by a garden. Charming, quirky and homely, the twenty-one individually decorated bedrooms match high ceilings with an earthy palette. The guesthouse also features a sunken living room with black leather couches and a large fireplace, and the quiet garden offers a peaceful break from the city centre. Their Irish breakfast is famed, as is their hospitality.

€€€

—

31 Leeson Close, Dublin 2
number31.ie
+353 1 676 5011

The Shelbourne

The Shelbourne is a landmark Dublin hotel with an enviable position
overlooking St Stephen's Green. The suites are warm and well appointed,
with décor perfectly befitting the two-hundred-year-old building, and
elsewhere there are various sophisticated spaces for rest, relaxation, and
revelry. The 27 Bar is bright and airy, with beautiful paintings that recall the
Green opposite; the Horseshoe Bar, with its rich dark wood and leather
has long been renowned as a meeting place for politicians and journalists.
For more wholesome pursuits, there is an excellent spa and pool, and an
elegant afternoon tea is served in the Lord Mayor's Lounge. With a top-level
restaurant, impeccable service, and an unparalleled location, the Shelbourne
is the perfect base for a five-star visit to Dublin.

€€€€

—

27 St Stephen's Green, Dublin 2
marriott.com/hotels/travel/dubbr-the-shelbourne-dublin-a-renaissance-hotel
+353 1 663 4500

Shops

Article

Article is only one of many reasons to visit the Powerscourt Townhouse Centre, a grand and beautiful Georgian building on South William Street, at the heart of Dublin's Creative Quarter. The building was once the city residence of Lord Powerscourt, but it has been developed into a bright and airy shopping centre with high-end boutiques, cafés, restaurants and a very fun bar (Pygmalion, pg. 105). Article opened its doors in 2010 and swiftly established itself as the go-to shop for high-end gifts, stationery and luxury homewares. Under its original eighteenth-century ceilings, you can browse the collection of contemporary prints, arty books, fine crockery and sumptuous textiles; everything in Article is functional and beautiful.

—

Powerscourt Townhouse Centre, South William Street, Dublin 2
articledublin.com
+353 1 679 9268

Brown Thomas

Located in a landmark building in the heart of Grafton Street, Brown Thomas is Dublin's pre-eminent luxury retailer, selling prêt-à-porter and haute couture clothing and accessories, menswear, children's clothes, homewares and beauty products over four levels. All the top international brands are represented, from Acqua di Parma to Yves Saint Laurent, and in addition Brown Thomas celebrates high-end Irish craft and design. The store frequently holds events, and the annual Create installation of Irish talent is a particular highlight. Brown Thomas offers tax-free shopping for international visitors, as well as personal shopping and grooming services, and a top-floor restaurant under the direction of chef Johnnie Cooke.

—

88-95 Grafton Street, Dublin 2
brownthomas.com
+353 1 605 6666

Fallon & Byrne

Spread over three floors – a basement wine bar, a ground-floor food hall and a second-floor restaurant – Fallon & Byrne is a foodie's paradise that prides itself on its artisan food, fine wine and top-tier service. The food hall is a great spot to find those trickier ingredients for a recipe, and it supplies discerning Dubliners and visitors with the best in fresh bread, cheese, meat and fish. For a quick lunch, pick up one of their delicious sandwiches or hot dishes from the deli counter. The wine bar downstairs has a laid-back but buzzing atmosphere and is a popular haunt with the after-work crowd. It serves an array of fantastic wines and a small food menu. Upstairs, you will find the more formal restaurant with classical French influences on the menu.

—

1-17 Exchequer Street, Dublin 2
fallonandbyrne.com
+353 1 472 1010

Folkster

Folkster is a vintage-inspired clothes boutique in Temple Bar, run by Irish stylist Blanaid Hennessy. It sells an eclectic array of women's day and evening wear, shoes, jewellery and a stylish homeware selection. The vibe is modern boho, with luxe fabrics and daring shapes in an array of cool, muted tones and the odd flash of sparkle. Entering off the cobbled street, the front room is packed with embellished pieces that are perfect for night-time, and in the back you'll find distinctive gowns for more special occasions, as well as interesting pieces for the home and a quirky range of cards and gifts. The friendly staff know their stuff and will happily give you a few pointers if asked.

—

9 Eustace Street, Temple Bar, Dublin 2
folkster.com
+353 1 675 0917

The Gutter Bookshop

When bookseller Bob Johnston made the brave decision to open an indie bookstore during a time when huge chain stores and on-line giants were ruling the book industry, he was inspired by the words of Oscar Wilde: 'We are all in the gutter, but some of us are looking at the stars.' This was in 2009, and the Gutter Bookshop is now a beloved Dublin institution, and a leading light in the city's literary scene. Situated on a charming little pedestrianised thoroughfare that runs from Dame Street to Temple Bar, the Gutter holds lots of launches, readings, and events, and the friendly, well-informed staff demonstrate a rich knowledge of the store's rigorously curated selection.

—

Cow's Lane, Temple Bar, Dublin 2
gutterbookshop.com
+353 1 679 9206

Hodges Figgis

Not many bookshops can boast of having been mentioned in James Joyce's *Ulysses*, but Hodges Figgis, Dublin's largest and oldest bookshop, has this claim to fame. Located on Dawson Street, very close to Trinity College (pg. 50) there are four floors of books of every genre, and like all good bookshops it has a large staff who know and love their books. Hodges Figgis has a particularly good Irish section, if you want to learn more about Ireland and its history, or to stock up on the works of Ireland's many famous writers. A long-established favourite amongst book-loving Dubliners.

—

56-58 Dawson Street, Dublin 2
waterstones.com/bookshops/hodges-figgis
+353 1 677 4754

Indigo & Cloth

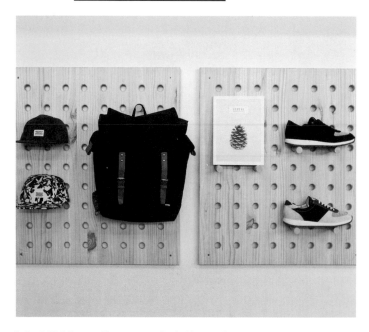

Indigo & Cloth is many things at once, all united by a modern design-led aesthetic and inspired by this quote from English mathematician G.H. Hardy: 'It is not worth an intelligent man's time to be in the majority. By definition, there are already enough people to do that.' The shop offers the coolest selection of menswear and accessories in town; there is a 'Brew Bar', which serves freshly brewed coffee in collaboration with Clement & Pekoe (pg. 79); and finally, the people behind the endeavour also operate as a creative agency. Come for the last word in cutting-edge brands, such as Baxter of California, INSTRMNT, Oliver Spencer, and Sandqvist, and their excellent selection of high-end international magazines.

—

9 Essex Street East, Dublin 2
indigoandcloth.com
+353 1 670 6403

<u>Industry</u>

In the heart of what has become known as the Creative Quarter, Industry is the coolest homewares shop in town. The aesthetic is Scandinavian industrial chic, as the name would suggest, and one gets the feeling that a lot of love has been put into the selection of their products. Expect rugs and pillows in soft neutral colours and distressed metal lamps with exposed lightbulbs. Recently they added a deli to the mix, and it quickly became equally popular. For a quick lunch, choose from their selection of healthy Middle-Eastern-inspired salads, served with grilled meat or fish.

—

41 Drury Street, Dublin 2
industryandco.com
+353 1 613 9111

Nowhere

Situated just slightly off the beaten shopping track, Nowhere carries a very carefully curated collection of 'extremely considered clothing', and the care taken does not end with the up-and-coming global menswear brands on sale. Shopping in Nowhere is a meticulously crafted experience, offering personal shopping, styling, and wardrobe maintenance, as well as the best magazines from around the world. Their philosophy is 'A shared curiosity in the discourse of masculinity and the culture of clothes', and this store is a required stop for the more discerning and adventurous fashionable man.

—

65 Aungier Street, Dublin 2
nowhere.ie
+353 1 607 8983

Parfumarija

If you are interested in rare and exclusive perfumes, this tiny boutique in the Westbury Mall, off Grafton Street, is an absolute must. In a clean, white and minimalist setting, it stocks a carefully selected range of niche brands of perfumes from all over the world, such as Frederic Malle and Molecule. There are also home fragrances, and face and body products. The owner, Marija Aslimoska, is a classically trained perfumier, so she knows her scents and will give you a little education on perfume if you ask for assistance.

—

25 Westbury Mall, Dublin 2
parfumarija.com
+353 1 671 0255

What to See

Guinness Storehouse

The Guinness Storehouse is Dublin's most popular tourist attraction, with almost 1.5 million visitors per year – and with good reason. The building, located in the heart of the St James's Gate Brewery, dates from 1904, but everything about the visitor experience is contemporary, as it charts the story of how Guinness is made and how it became a global phenomenon. Great care has been taken with the attraction's execution and upkeep, and the tour is slick and inventive; it begins at the bottom of a giant pint glass and ascends seven storeys. Admission is €14 for an adult, and this includes a free pint of 'The Black Stuff' in the Storehouse's crowning glory, the Gravity Bar, which offers unparalleled 360-degree views of the city.

—

St James's Gate, Dublin 8
guinness-storehouse.com
+353 1 408 4800

IMMA

Located in the Royal Hospital Kilmainham, and surrounded by sprawling gardens, the exciting collection of the Irish Museum of Modern Art is at odds with its distinguished exterior. Inside, contemporary works by established artists and up-and-comers are displayed. Exhibitions usually last three to four months, so check online to see what's on.

—

Military Road, Dublin 8
imma.ie
+353 1 612 9900

Kilmain-
ham
Gaol

Take the Number 13 or 40 bus (both
leave frequently from Dame Street) for
the fifteen-minute journey to the historic
Kilmainham Gaol. The truly excellent tour of
the prison is a crash-course in Irish history,
particularly the tragic and bitter struggle
for independence from the British Empire.
Kilmainham has a long and significant history
but it is most famous as the location of the
execution of several of the rebels behind the
1916 Easter Rising. These executions caused
such outrage that they are considered
the trigger for the War of Independence
which ultimately led to the separation of the
Republic of Ireland from the British Empire.
The building is fascinating and has been used
as the setting for many films, including *In the
Name of the Father* and *The Italian Job*.

—

Inchicore Road, Kilmainham, Dublin 8
kilmainhamgaolmuseum.ie
+353 1 453 5984

National Gallery

The National Gallery boasts a vast and fascinating collection of Irish and European art. There are a number of stand-out pieces, perhaps most notably Caravaggio's 'The Taking of Christ', in which the chiaroscuro method is used to mesmerising effect. The collection of Irish artworks (especially those of Jack B. Yeats, William Orpen and Louis le Brocquy) is also excellent. The building alone makes it worth a visit, as the grand original gallery merges with the very modern wing that opens onto Clare Street (near Trinity College, at the end of Nassau Street).

—

Merrion Square West, Dublin 2
nationalgallery.ie
+353 1 661 5133

National Museum

The National Museum of Ireland has three locations in Dublin, and in the Kildare Street branch the focus is on archaeology, although you don't have to be an expert in the field to appreciate the exhibits on view here. This beautiful space is home to a vibrant collection of archaeological treasures and priceless pieces that tell the stories of ancient Ireland and its people. The most significant artefacts in the seven galleries include the Tara Brooch, the Ardagh Chalice, and the 'Bog Bodies', a recent haunting addition of preserved bodies from the Iron Age.

—

Kildare Street, Dublin 2
museum.ie
+353 1 6777444

Natural History Museum

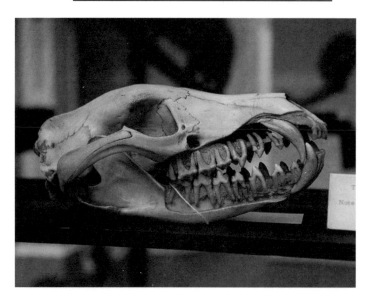

The Natural History Museum, known affectionately as 'The Dead Zoo', is a branch of the National Museum of Ireland that is dedicated to zoology. Located beside Government Buildings, it dates from 1857 and is a fine example of a Victorian cabinet-style museum. Indeed, entering is like walking into the past. Little has changed with the static menagerie in the last century; some of the animals show scars from bullet holes and evidence of the rudimentary nature of Victorian taxidermy. The ground floor is dedicated to Irish wildlife, and the second floor is home to myriad exotic animals, including a dodo skeleton. A fascinating, fun, and occasionally haunting experience.

—

Merrion Street Upper, Dublin 2
museum.ie
+353 1 6777444

Temple Bar

Temple Bar is often dismissed as a tourist trap, but a trip to Dublin would be incomplete without a visit and today it does hold some gems. Cross the Ha'penny Bridge then enter through the cobbled Merchant's Arch and enjoy the very lively square. On Saturdays, you can browse the book stalls, and then head for the food market in Meeting House Square (pg. 114), where you must try a fresh oyster with a swig of white wine. We recommend Klaw (pg. 64) for lunch, then a browse in the Temple Bar Gallery, the Library Project, or the Gallery of Photography. In the evening, the Porterhouse offers good traditional music and its own craft beers.

—

Dublin 2
dublin.info/temple-bar

Trinity
College

Trinity College is the *alma mater* of Jonathan Swift, Oscar Wilde and Samuel Beckett, and its campus, in the very centre of Dublin, is an embarrassment of riches. The Long Room Library, a stunning sight in its own right, is home to the Book of Kells, a ninth-century manuscript that is undoubtedly one of Ireland's greatest treasures. Queues can be long, so book a fast-track ticket online in advance. For a contemporary contrast, the Science Gallery is an excellent, compact and interactive attraction that is well worth a visit. In nice weather, the cricket pavilion – known locally as 'the Pav'– attracts the sun long into the evening, and with it, hordes of young professionals who wind down *al fresco*.

—

College Green, Dublin 2
tcd.ie
+353 1 896 1000

Restau-
rants

777

You could easily miss the dark plain exterior of contemporary
Mexican restaurant 777, but open the door and you'll be hit
with a punch of colour and noise, as diners enjoy margaritas
against a backdrop of painted tile and dripping candles.
777 offers a wide range of fish and meat dishes, alongside
an impressive cocktail and tequila list. We recommend the
tostados and taquitos, which are perfect for sharing and
for sampling as many flavours as possible. Sundays offer a
spin on the traditional brunch menu, with dishes and special
cocktails all priced at €7.77. Bookings are for parties of six
or more only, otherwise it's first come first served. Parties of
two are seated along the bar, but the buzzing atmosphere
makes this a fun date venue.

€€€

—

Castle House, South Great George's Street, Dublin 2
777.ie
+353 1 425 4052

Bastible

Situated a little off the beaten track, in the bustling Dublin 8 area, this contemporary bistro is worth seeking out. It gets its name from a type of pot that was used for baking in nineteenth-century Ireland, and every day here they use modern replicas to bake fermented sourdough bread that will later be served with homemade butter. This sums up the ethos at Bastible: high-quality Irish ingredients sourced from artisan producers transformed by modern cooking that has a forensic attention to detail. The interior has something of a masculine feel, but it's still warm and intimate. While the friendly staff do their best to accommodate walk-ins, we recommend that you book in advance, as Bastible's reputation has quickly made these among the most sought-after tables in town.

€€€€

—

11 South Circular Road, Dublin 2
bastible.com
+353 1 473 7409

Bunsen

The Bunsen menu is the size of a business card. There, you will find four variations on the traditional burger (hamburger or cheeseburger, single or double), classic toppings (you won't find blue cheese or hummus here) and three types of fries. This is the genius of Bunsen. It offers good-value food, cooked to order, and the concise menu instils complete confidence in the quality of ingredients. Black Aberdeen Angus beef, supplied by famed Dublin butcher FX Buckley, is minced freshly each morning, and the buns are made to order by a County Dublin bakery daily. Bookings are only accepted for groups of eight to ten, but with three locations, all within a stone's throw of the Creative Quarter, you should have no problem getting a Bunsen burger fix.

€

—

36 Wexford Street, 22 Essex Street East, 3 Anne Street South, Dublin 2
Bunsen.ie
+353 1 559 9532 (Essex St)

Coppinger Row

Coppinger Row hit the national headlines in 2016 when it was the dinner choice of Beyoncé and Jay Z, but in Dublin it is perhaps best known as one of the city's premier brunch spots. Its cool interior, amiable service and, crucially, its Blood Marys, make this the perfect hangover venue. The black pudding salad, and the wild mushroom with asparagus, poached egg and hollandaise, are stand-outs. Blankets are provided for those seated on the terrace, and its location, on a side street between busy thoroughfares, makes it a desirable people-watching spot. There are no reservations for parties of fewer than six, so get there early for dinner.

€€€

—

1 Coppinger Row, Dublin 2
coppingerrow.com
+353 1 672 9884

Cotto

The stripped-back interior of Cotto reflects owner and chef Conor Higgins' ethos of 'less is more'. His cooking style is understated but accomplished, as reflected in the pizza menu, which features trusted favourites like the Napoli and Diavolo (we recommend the Elliot, with fennel sausage, baby kale, ricotta and chilli oil). The mouthwatering traditional Neopolitan pizzas are contrasted with dips and lighter seasonal sides, like heritage beetroot *agro dolce*, and interesting specials, such as chargrilled octopus with ruby grapefruit. There are good vegetarian options and the kitchen is very happy to accommodate vegans. Cotto pizzas are now available to takeaway, and it is also a popular spot for lunch during the week and brunch at weekends.

€€

—

46 Manor Street, Stoneybatter, Dublin 7
cotto.ie
+353 1 552 2918

Delahunt

At a time when many eateries are still looking to our
Northern European cousins for inspiration, Delahunt is
a breath of fresh air, both in terms of food and interior
design. Painstakingly and lovingly restored over a period
of eighteen months, this building originally housed a high-
end grocer namechecked by James Joyce in *Ulysses*.
In the upstairs cocktail bar, the huge bay window opens
wide onto busy Camden Street, and downstairs, the
elegant dining room, with its high ceiling and white
marble, serves an inspiring menu of contemporary Irish
cuisine, where classic Irish elements like cockles and
mussels, smoked eel and Guinness bread are employed
in exciting, modern dishes.

€€€€

—

39 Camden Street Lower, Dublin 2
delahunt.ie
+353 1 598 4880

Etto

In Italian 'etto' means 100 grams and tends to be the unit most commonly used in markets to measure produce. This reflects Etto's emphasis on sourcing quality ingredients and the fact that the food is Mediterranean with an Italian accent. Critics and locals alike have been raving about this little gem since it opened in Dublin's business district, a few minutes' walk from St Stephen's Green. Etto is set in a simple room with a bar at the back; its food menu, divided into 'small plates' and 'large plates', is short and changes daily, and the wine menu is extensive. The food is innovative and truly delicious, and a giant step from the 'spag bol' Italian restaurants of the not-too-distant past.

€€€

—

18 Merrion Row, Dublin 2
etto.ie
+353 1 678 8872

Fade Street Social

Fade Street Social certainly lives up to the 'social' in its name, as it is friendly, buzzy and crowded, and the sort of place where you often end up chatting to the people seated beside you. Downstairs comprises a gastro bar with sharing platters and tapas-style dishes, and a restaurant with a more formal seating arrangement and menu. Upstairs there's a cocktail bar and a 'Winter Garden' where you can sip on a cocktail *al fresco* – smokers take note. Despite the hipness of the venue, what is actually most impressive about Fade Street Social is the food. Chef Dylan McGrath focuses on homegrown fresh ingredients and creates interesting and modern dishes that are appealing and delicious. Try the pumpkin ravioli from the tapas menu.

€€€

—

6 Fade St, Dublin 2
fadestreetsocial.com
+353 1 604 0066

Forest Avenue

Opened in 2013 by husband and wife team John and Sandy Wyer, Forest Avenue quickly established itself as one of Dublin's best restaurants. The couple modestly term it 'a neighbourhood dining room', but this is unquestionably haute cuisine. Chef John says, 'I like food that has been considered, that isn't overcomplicated or overworked, and uses good ingredients', and Irish ingredients are always key to his ever-changing menu. The consensus is that Forest Avenue is excellent value; Michelin-star quality at less than the usual prices. The space is sparse but inviting, with Scandinavian overtones, and the staff are extremely welcoming. If you can get a table, you're likely to be sharing the dining room with some of Dublin's other high-profile chefs.

€€€€

—

8 Sussex Terrace, Dublin 4
forestavenuerestaurant.ie
+353 1 667 8337

Klaw

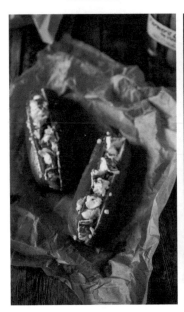

For a city right on the sea, until recently Dublin had a strange
dearth of seafood restaurants. All that has changed, of late, and
seafood is having something of a moment, with eateries (both
formal and casual) popping up around the city where fish is most
certainly centre stage. Right in the middle of the action in Temple
Bar, Klaw is a chilled and super-cool seafood shack. There's not
much to it: a few wooden benches and a giant blackboard, but
the hipster in you will delight in the industrial chic details such
as the filament lightbulbs and the chowder served in tin cans.
Apart from the chowder, it's shellfish all the way, with Galway Bay
Oysters washed down with a glass of Guinness or Prosecco, or
lobster served on buttery brioche rolls.

€

—

5A Crown Alley, Temple Bar, Dublin 2
klaw.ie
+353 1 549 3443

Luna

Luna is part of a collection of restaurants at this Drury Street
address. Super Miss Sue is a seafood restaurant, Cervi is
the most hipster fish-and-chip joint in the city, and Luna is
the sophisticated older sister located in the basement. It
began with a lot of fanfare and managed to win the Best Irish
Restaurant Award within a year of its opening. It is definitely
the most formal of the three, but the retro Italian-American
menu (think high-end prawn cocktail with avocado) and
kitsch interiors (soft lighting, Campari advertisements and
dark leather booths), harking back to the 1960s, make Luna
a stylish, fun and memorable dinner destination. It's an
extremely popular spot, so be sure to book.

€€€€

—

2-3 Drury Street, Dublin 2
supermisssue.com/luna
+353 1 679 9009

Musashi

Musashi has a devoted fan base, with Dubliners coming in their droves for the delicious fresh sushi, the wide range of hot Japanese dishes, and for the lunchtime bento boxes. The friendly staff, pared-back interior and soft lighting create a relaxed atmosphere and put the food in the spotlight. The spicy tuna rolls and the gyoza are not to be missed. The food is reasonably priced, and you can bring your own wine (€6 corkage), which just adds to Musashi's charm. This is the perfect spot for dinner before hitting the nearby pubs, but don't be surprised if you find you're enjoying yourself so much you don't want to leave. Booking is advised, particularly at weekends.

€

—

15 Capel Street, Dublin 1
musashidublin.com
+353 1 532 8057

Patrick Guilbaud

Restaurant Patrick Guilbaud is Ireland's only restaurant with two Michelin stars. Opened in 1981, it is located in the Merrion Hotel (pg. 20), across the road from the Dáil (the lower house of parliament), so you are likely to be sitting beside one of Ireland's ministers or a visiting celebrity. The food is classical, using the finest in Irish ingredients, and very nouvelle cuisine in terms of portion sizes and presentation. There are a number of menu variations available to suit any occasion, from the two-course Table d'Hote lunch menu to the eight-course Degustation dinner menu. The interiors are subdued and confident, the wine list is immense, and the service is famed for its precision and impeccable attention to detail.

€€€€+

—

21 Upper Merrion Street, Dublin 2
restaurantpatrickguilbaud.ie
+353 1 676 4192

Pickle

Since Pickle opened its doors in 2016, it has been receiving rave reviews, and with good reason. With exposed brickwork and kitsch Indian art on the walls, the inviting interiors serve only as a backdrop to the star of the show: the sophisticated Indian cuisine. With chef Sunil Ghai at the helm, and professional and polite floor staff, Pickle provides innovative yet unpretentious food that is just delicious. The fantastic tiffin boxes served at lunchtime, with smallish helpings of a number of dishes, are also a quick and reasonable way to enjoy this restaurant's amazing food. It's popular and very busy at night, so book ahead.

€€€

—

43 Camden Street, Dublin 2
picklerestaurant.com
+353 1 555 7755

Skinflint

On a quiet laneway just off Dame Street, the main
artery that runs from Christchurch to Trinity College,
Skinflint is a casual and trendy spot, perfect for
grabbing a quick bite before a night out. The décor
is classic hipster; dimly lit, with big wooden tables
and high stools (be prepared to get cosy with your
neighbours at busier times) and toilets wallpapered
with retro posters. The scrumptious pizzas are fresh,
generous in size, and nicely accompanied by a good
range of craft beers and tasty cocktails. The lunch
menu is also a winner, with the sinfully delicious
sandwiches served in bread pockets made from pizza
dough. Veggie and healthy options galore.

€

—

Crane Lane, Dublin 2
joburger.ie/skinflint
+353 1 670 9719

Taste at Rustic

Chef Dylan McGrath is something of celebrity in Dublin; he has been awarded Michelin stars, he appears regularly on television, and he has created a restaurant empire in the city (see Fade Street Social, pg. 61). Taste, situated above Rustic Stone, is his latest project, and is said to be inspired by his global travels and specifically by cuisine from Japan, Spain and South America. The Japanese influence is immediately evident when you open the large menu, which is divided into sweet, sour, salt, bitter, and umami. The food is elegant, inventive and delicious, with a wide range of sushi, robata-grilled meats, and Nabemono broths.

€€€€

—

17 South Great George's Street, Dublin 2
tasteatrusticstone.com
+353 1 526 7701

The Vintage Kitchen

What the Vintage Kitchen lacks in size, it make up for in charm. It has a homely feeling and a refreshing lack of studied self-consciousness, with relaxed interiors and vintage art and crafts on show. Here, the focus is on good, honest food. The menu is bursting with exquisite interpretations of classic comfort-food dishes, showcasing top-quality ingredients. Combine with a visit to the neighbouring Mulligan's pub (pg. 93), and don't forget your vinyl – as well as a BYOB policy (with no corkage fees), the Vintage Kitchen operates a 'Bring Your Own LP' service, so you can listen to your favourite music while you dine. Booking is strongly advised.

€€€

—

7 Poolbeg Street, Dublin 2
thevintagekitchen.ie
+353 1 679 8705

The Winding Stair

The Winding Stair restaurant is located above the delightful bookshop of the same name, up a creaky set of stairs and on the first floor overlooking the River Liffey. The interior dispenses with the fuss: with white walls and exposed pipes, simplicity is the key. The à la carte menu changes daily and focuses on Irish-sourced ingredients from quality suppliers, with the provenance of the meat and seafood listed with the ingredients. The food is wholesome and delicious, and the atmosphere is warm and unpretentious; it's easy to see why it's a favourite among many locals. For the best value, arrive early mid-week and try the pre-theatre menu before heading to a show at the nearby Gate or Abbey Theatres.

€€€

—

40 Lower Ormond Quay, Dublin 1
winding-stair.com
+353 1 872 7320

Wuff

Not far from both Smithfield and Stoneybatter, Wuff is a trendy neighbourhood bistro sitting in a corner building alongside the Luas lines on Dublin's Northside. The iron-framed windows and grey walls give the interiors a bit of a cool warehouse vibe, and yet Wuff is as friendly and welcoming as they come. The bistro menu is reasonable and hearty – try the juicy burger and thick-cut sweet potato fries done to perfection. It's also a great place for brunch before a day of sightseeing.

€€

—

23 Benburb Street, Dublin 7
wuff.ie
+353 1 532 0347

Cafés

3FE

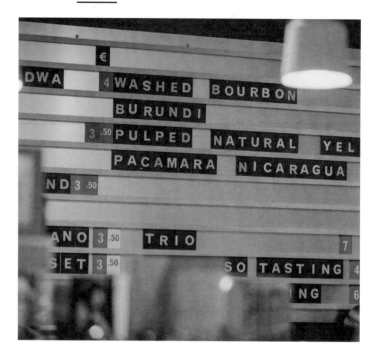

If you are the sort that takes your coffee as seriously as you take your wine, then 3FE should be on your list of cafés in Dublin to visit. Their coffee is so good that they supply many of the eateries in the city with their beans. The humble food menu makes for a quick and easy lunch, but it plays second fiddle to the coffee tasting menu, which includes a 'coffee trio' (coffee served three ways). The owner, Colin Harmon, left his job in the finance world to become an award-winning barista, and has since focused on his ever-growing coffee empire.

—

32 Grand Canal Street Lower, Dublin 2
3FE.com
+353 1 661 9329

Clement & Pekoe

Clement & Pekoe is one of the many eateries on the trendy South William Street in the heart of what has been branded the Creative Quarter of the city. The little café is known for baked goods and pastries, and the select range of coffees and loose-leaf teas that you can purchase to bring home with you. On a sunny day you can sit outside on one of the benches and people-watch. Otherwise, sit inside and enjoy the elegant interiors.

—

50 South William Street, Dublin 2
clementandpekoe.com
info@clementandpekoe.com

The Fumbally

The warm environment and welcoming staff at the Fumbally reflect that this café is a labour of love. Its owners, Aisling Rogerson and Luca D'Alfonso, have spoken about how much they value its place in the community, and this general sense of consideration is evident everywhere. Slightly off the beaten track, it's a short walk from St Patrick's Cathedral, and visitors are rewarded with a bright, airy room with an impressively high ceiling, eclectic furniture, and enticing displays of produce. The menu is reassuringly precise, with salads changing daily and cakes baked in-house, and there is a focus on organic, local and ethical ingredients. Coffee is provided by 3FE and by a rotation of guest roasters, and so flavours change from season to season, meaning there is always an excuse to return.

—

Fumbally Lane, Dublin 8
thefumbally.ie
+353 1 529 8732

Kaph

Located in the middle of Dublin's Creative Quarter, Kaph is a stand-out city centre café. Its minimalist interior is sophisticated and sleek, and while the aesthetic is effortless, the care taken with the coffee is anything but. The knowledgeable, good-humoured staff prepare the highest-quality coffees (roasts by 3FE, with beans available to take away) and offer a range of treats, including Paleo cakes, all at reasonable prices. Upstairs there is an art and event space, and the window displays by local illustrators always raise a smile. The cushioned window seat (or, on warmer days, the little bench outside) is the ideal spot to watch the world go by.

—

31 Drury Street, Dublin 2
kaph.ie
+353 1 613 9030

Two Boys Brew

The Two Boys in question – Kevin Roche and Taurean Coughlan – have backgrounds in design and media respectively, and this expertise has certainly enhanced their contribution to Dublin's café culture. This tasteful space – pared back, with industrial colours, pops of greenery, and flooded with natural light – and exquisitely curated range of international magazines make this a relaxing space, even when packed to capacity. The delicious dishes are presented beautifully, and service is remarkably friendly and efficient. Alongside the lunch menu, brunch is served all day every day. A perfect stop *en route* to the nearby Glasnevin Cemetery and Botanical Gardens, be prepared to queue on weekends – it's worth the wait.

—

375 North Circular Road, Dublin 7
twoboysbrew.ie
info@twoboysbrew.ie

Brother Hubbard

Capel Street has come up in the world over the last number of years and now boasts some of the coolest pubs, restaurants and cafés in town. Brother Hubbard is no exception, and is often packed with locals chatting over coffee. They are proud of their locally sourced tea and coffee, but what really separates this casual eatery from its competitors is the food. The brunch is the stuff of dreams and the reasonably priced Middle-Eastern feast for dinner has created something of a frenzy amongst Dubliners on the look out for something new. Unlike the claggy, oily fare that is often dubbed Middle Eastern, at Brother Hubbard, the humble falafel, beef meatballs, and 'wedding' couscous taste incredibly fresh and delicious, and will leave you wondering what on earth they do to make the food taste so good.

—

153 Capel Street, Dublin 1
brotherhubbard.ie
+353 1 441 1112

Pubs

Grogan's

Appearing in Flann O'Brien's 1939 novel *At Swim-Two-Birds*, Grogan's later became a haunt of leading figures of the Irish literati, such as Patrick Kavanagh, J.P. Donleavy and Liam O'Flaherty. Not much has changed, and the pub's traditional atmosphere is as 'Dublin' as it comes. The walls are lined with pieces of art, which are sold off twice a year, and a large outdoor seating area is perfect for people-watching when the sun is shining. Book launches and poetry readings are also common, as Grogan's stays true to its literary heritage. You won't find craft beers or cocktail menus here, but stop by for a delicious pint of Guinness, one of their famous ham-and-cheese toasties, and a real Dublin-pub experience.

—

15 South William Street, Dublin 2
groganspub.ie
+353 1 677 9320

The Hacienda

The Hacienda is unquestionably one of Dublin's best-kept secrets. An unassuming whitewashed exterior, located off lively Capel Street and close to the fruit and vegetable market, belies an intimate, eclectic pub that is frequented by the city's A-list visitors, who play pool and listen to the jukebox till the early hours. Visitors must ring a doorbell for admittance, which is granted by the owner, Shay, so if you meet with his approval you are guaranteed a relaxed and fun evening. Hours are changeable, but it generally opens at 8pm. We recommend that you arrive early to secure a table, and enjoy the gradual flow of interesting arrivals.

—

15 Little Mary Street, Dublin 1
+353 1 873 0535

Kehoe's

First licensed in 1803, Kehoe's retains a Victorian-style interior that
brings visitors back in time, with its grocery counter, mahogany
partitions, vintage advertising and authentic furniture. Patrick
Kavanagh, Brendan Behan and Flann O'Brien were regulars here,
even if they were not always warmly welcomed by the conservative
proprietor, John Kehoe. Today, it's a buzzing city-centre pub that offers
a glimpse into a Dublin of old, but sports fans and the after-work crowd
keep it grounded in the present. The many snugs are almost always
occupied at busy periods, but if you get a chance, slip in and take note
of the Victorian serving hatch and buzzer. When there is sunshine –
even a sliver – an amiable crowd spills onto the street outside.

—

9 South Anne Street, Dublin 2
louisfitzgerald.com/kehoes
+353 1 677 8312

L. Mulligan. Grocer

As the name would suggest, this Dublin pub was formerly a grocer's shop. It's now known as Mulligan's, and is a cosy and buzzy spot in the fashionable neighbourhood of Stoneybatter. As well as having large selections of craft beers and whiskies, the seasonal food menu is fantastic, which is a rare find in Dublin pubs. Offering pub-grub classics such as lamb burgers and fish and chips alongside potted crab, vegetarian haggis, and steaming bowls of mussels, the quality is the consistent factor. The staff and clientele are friendly and cheerful, making this a great place to relax with a drink, lunch and the weekend papers.

—

18 Stoneybatter, Dublin 7
lmulligangrocer.com
+353 1 670 9889

The Long Hall

On Dublin's busy South Great George's Street (locally known as George's Street) stands this charming and intimate Victorian relic, open since 1766. It has retained much of its old-fashioned interiors and has some of the friendliest and most helpful bar staff in Dublin. Come early and be prepared to share a table as this place gets very crowded. Creamy pints of Guinness and a fantastic pub atmosphere; you can't ask for much more from a traditional Dublin pub. Bruce Springsteen has called the Long Hall his 'Dublin local', and fans of Thin Lizzy's Phil Lynott will recognise it from the video for his classic song 'Old Town'.

—

51 South Great George' Street, Dublin 2
+353 1 475 1590

Mulligan's

Established almost 300 years ago, Mulligan's
moved to its current building in 1854. Dark
mahogany furniture and embossed wallpapers
bring customers back in time as soon as they
step through the door. Celebrated customers
have included Judy Garland, Seamus Heaney
and John F. Kennedy, and the pub featured in
James Joyce's famed short-story collection,
Dubliners. Like many Dublin pubs, there are
various snugs, and nooks and crannies where
you can take up residence for the evening.

—

8 Poolbeg Street, Dublin 2
mulligans.ie
+353 1 677 5582

O'Donoghue's

Another of the oldest establishments in Dublin, O'Donoghue's opened as a grocer's in 1789 and became a licensed pub in 1943. Many notable musicians have performed here over the years, including legendary folk group The Dubliners, singer Christy Moore, and Thin Lizzy frontman Phil Lynott. It's a very short stroll from St Stephen's Green and still offers live music seven nights a week, so be sure to visit for a drink and to hear some excellent traditional musicians. Located as it is on the edge of one of the city's main business districts, and boasting one of its best smoking areas, O'Donoghue's attracts a lively after-work crowd – a great way to start a night on the town.

—

15 Merrion Row Dublin 2
odonoghues.ie
+353 1 660 7194

The Stag's Head

A restored mosaic on the Dame Street pavement leads the way along a narrow alley to this Victorian pub tucked away on Dame Lane. The interior is crowned by a stuffed stag's head which looks down on locals and tourists alike, while a mahogany bar, marble floors, and granite tabletops enhance the atmosphere. The founder's name can still be seen on the large clock outside the building, which dates from 1894. While traditional on the inside, the Stag's Head regularly hosts comedy nights and live music, poetry and spoken-word events. This is an extremely popular spot, so come early to get a seat. In better weather, the fun spills out onto Dame Lane, which is crowded and lively in the summertime.

—

1 Dame Court, Dublin 2
louisfitzgerald.com/stagshead
+353 1 679 3687

Bars
& Clubs

The Bernard Shaw

Don't let the tumbledown exterior fool you – inside, the Bernard Shaw is a quirky space filled with colourful artwork, playing indie music, and serving a great selection of drinks, including craft beers. It attracts a friendly alternative crowd and can get very busy at the weekends. The beer garden out the back is perfect for a pint in the sun, and, as with many smoking areas in Dublin, it gets more fun as the night wears on. The outdoor area is also host to a double-decker blue bus, from which you can order a freshly made pizza.

—

11-12 Richmond Street South, Dublin 2
bodytonicmusic.com/thebernardshaw
+353 1 906 0218

The Chelsea Drugstore

You can't miss the Chelsea Drugstore, located on bustling George's Street, with its striking sign composed of white lightbulbs. The original Chelsea Drugstore was a shopping mall in London in the 1960s, famously namechecked in the Rolling Stones hit 'You Can't Always Get What You Want'. Here, however, you'll find a modern and cosy bar with an impressive menu comprising an extensive cocktail list, craft beers, and a selection of wines and gins. The vibe is laid back and mellow with a sophisticated art deco element to the interior.

—

25 South Great George's Street, Dublin 2
thechelseadrugstore.ie
+353 1 613 9093

The Dice Bar

The Dice Bar isn't your standard local pub, but it's the right one for this location, just a stone's throw from the alternative havens of Smithfield and Stoneybatter. A dive bar that wouldn't look out of place in New York, the black walls and seats, dark red ceiling and ephemera-scattered walls are contrasted with vast windows overlooking the Luas line, making this the perfect day-to-night bar. An impressive selection of craft beers (including home brews) and DJs at the weekend draw big crowds that often trickle out onto the wide corner pavement.

—

79 Queen Street, Dublin 7
dicebar.com
+353 1 633 3936

Mother

Mother is a gay, straight-friendly club night that is one of best of its kind in Ireland. Held every Saturday from 11pm, it specialises in disco, electro and synth-pop, and each week it is a joyous celebration of music and dancing. Originally conceived as a way to fundraise for Dublin's *GCN* (*Gay Community News*) magazine, the club's popularity has grown so much that they now perform sets at Ireland's biggest music festivals, throw a block party that is the annual highlight of Pride, and support superstars like Grace Jones in concert. €10; over 21s only.

—

23 Eustace Street, Dublin 2
motherclub.ie
+353 1 670 8777

No Name Bar

Even though no one seems entirely sure what to call this place, it's a bar with which all Dubliners are familiar. It's one of many well-established haunts on Fade Street, situated above L'Gueuleton Restaurant, in a restored Victorian townhouse that is also home to Kelly's Hotel (pg. 18). The interiors are uber-hip; three huge rooms are filled with large sofas, battered mismatched furniture and art on the walls, giving the place a loft feel. It gets noisy and busy, and there's no shortage of atmosphere, attracting a mixed, slightly upmarket crowd. There's also a huge outdoor seating area, and it serves top-quality cocktails until late.

—

3 Fade Street, Dublin 2
nonamebardublin.com
+353 87 122 1064

P. Mac's

P. Mac's prides itself on the wide range of craft beers available, many of them locally brewed, and the staff certainly know what's what when it comes to beer. It's a cosy, busy joint with great little snugs, shabby-chic lampshades and mismatched furniture. With its board games, bookshelves, candles on tables, and old-school bags of crisps, it's all achingly retro, but it definitely works, and discerning grungy Dubliners flock here in their droves in the evenings. The menu is quick and reasonable and perfect for a quick bite if you're too busy enjoying the craic to look for a restaurant. Try the fish tacos.

—

28-30 Stephen Street Lower, Dublin 2
facebook.com/pmacspub/
+353 1 475 8578

PantiBar

Run by Ireland's premiere drag queen Panti Bliss – who came to international attention during the Marriage Equality referendum – neon-tinted PantiBar is a favoured haunt of Dublin's LGBT community. There are karaoke nights, pub quizzes, lots of dancing, and friendly and fun staff. If you want a quiet drink, call in to try their cocktails on a weekday, because at the weekend, PantiBar doesn't hold back. Saturday nights are particularly raucous; if you're lucky you might catch a performance by Panti herself.

—

7-8 Capel Street, Dublin 1
pantibar.com
+353 1 874 0710

Pygmalion

Located on the corner of the Powerscourt Shopping Centre and along the picturesque South William Street, Pygmalion doubles as a café and restaurant during the day and a lively club at night. Also known as PYG, the high stone walls, bronze bathrooms and muted colour scheme give the place a stylish vibe. The club frequently hosts Irish and international DJs, so prepare to get cosy on the dancefloor at night. Their outdoor area is perfectly placed for people-watching, and on Sundays they offer great deals on food and drinks – get there before 4pm for free admission.

—

59 South William Street, Dublin 2
Pyg.ie
+353 1 633 4522

The Liquor Rooms

The Liquor Rooms are easy to walk past, nestled as they are underneath the Clarence Hotel on Wellington Quay. Descend the steps, however, and you'll find a speakeasy-style subterranean bar that serves cutting-edge cocktails and plays quality music. With circus-inspired décor, red velvet drapes and dim lighting, you'd be forgiven for expecting a burlesque show to start at any minute. Instead, this club often runs literary events, spoken-word performances and cocktail tastings. In true speakeasy style, this club gets warm and close, so emerging back onto the busy Dublin quays at the end of the night can be quite a shock to the system.

—

5 Wellington Quay, Dublin 2
theliquorrooms.com
+353 87 339 3688

The Workman's Club

The Workman's Club opened its doors in 2010. It is situated in a beautiful building dating from 1888 on the edge of Temple Bar, beside the famous Clarence Hotel and looking onto the Liffey, and Dubliners head here when they want to continue the fun after a few in one of the nearby pubs. Its live music offerings also draw big crowds (Dan le Sac Vs Scroobius Pip, Future Islands, Imelda May, Little Green Cars, and Father John Misty have all played here). Attracting a diverse clientele, this multi-floor venue is big, busy, noisy, fun and stays open late.

—

10 Wellington Quay, Dublin 2
theworkmansclub.com
+353 1 670 6692

Markets

Ha'Penny Flea

Situated at the north end of the Ha'Penny Bridge, the Grand Social is a bar, club and live music venue. Its Parlour bar looks out onto the rush of foot traffic towards the bridge, and later in the evenings the Ballroom, Loft and Roof Garden offer a wide range of entertainment. Every Saturday, the Grand Social hosts the Ha'Penny Vintage & Craft Market. The offerings change every week, with a wide range of jewellery, vintage clothes, vinyl, books and art on sale. With DJs playing great music, this is an ideal location for an afternoon browse with a coffee, or something stronger.

Saturday, 12pm to 6pm.

—

The Grand Social, 35 Liffey Street Lower, Dublin 1
thegrandsocial.ie/market/
+353 1 873 4332

Moore Street

Situated a short walk from the Spire, Moore Street is a bustling slice of authentic Dublin and an area of some historical significance, as leaders of the 1916 Easter Rising surrendered from houses here. Today, the street is somewhat rough around the edges but always buzzing, thanks to its market of fruit, vegetables, flowers and fish. This is the oldest market in the city, and many of the stalls have been in the same families for generations. The traders are formidable Dublin characters who are quick with a smile and a joke, but be warned, they don't like customers touching their produce to test for ripeness, so do so at your peril. Aside from the market, the street is lively and multicultural, with a number of ethnic grocers and inexpensive restaurants.

Monday to Saturday, 8am to 5pm.

—

Moore Street, Dublin 1

Temple Bar Food Market

Tucked away off the cobbled streets of Temple Bar, Meeting House Square is a quaint space that hosts lots of events throughout the year. With the installation of a retractable roof, the square branded itself 'Dublin's Outdoor, Indoor Space' and its weekly food market, held every Saturday from 10am to 4.30pm, is beloved by tourists and Dubliners alike. Friendly food producers and street food vendors travel weekly to sell their wares, and the quality is exceptional, with fresh fruit and vegetables, artisan meats and cheeses, and delicious bread and cakes. If you can't wait until you get home, there's a great range of international snacks and hot meals on offer; try some fresh oysters with tabasco and a sip of cold white wine.

Saturday, 10.30am to 4pm.

—

Meeting House Square, Dublin 2
facebook.com/TempleBarFoodMarket
+353 1 677 2255

Parks

Iveagh Gardens

Tucked between St Stephen's Green, bustling Harcourt Street and the National Concert Hall, the Iveagh Gardens are sometimes referred to as the city's 'secret garden'. A quiet pocket of calm, it is a more rustic park than its city centre counterparts, and the abundant greenery is punctuated by two stunning fountains and a dramatic cascade, formed by rocks from Ireland's thirty-two counties. Open to the public according to daylight hours, the Iveagh Gardens is an ideal spot for a picnic or some sunshine reading, and it hosts a number of evening events throughout the year, including comedy festivals and open-air concerts.

Monday to Saturday, 8am to dusk (6pm, March to October).

—

Clonmel St, Off Harcourt St, Dublin 2
www.iveaghgardens.ie

Merrion Square

St Stephen's Green, with its position at the top of bustling Grafton Street, is often lauded as city's best cultivated park, but Merrion Square is a calm and lush oasis of colour in the heart of Georgian Dublin. On a sunny day it is the perfect place to relax, maybe after a visit to the adjacent National Gallery (pg. 46) or Natural History Museum (pg. 48), and during the summer, local artists display their paintings on the park's margins. Oscar Wilde once lived in a house overlooking the square, so be sure to visit his statue, which boasts perhaps the smuggest expression ever carved in stone. A fitting tribute.

Monday to Sunday, 10am to sunset (10pm in summer).

—

Merrion Square, Dublin 2
merrionsquare.ie

Phoenix Park

The largest enclosed park in Europe, Phoenix Park was first conceived as a deer park, and still retains a large herd of its original tenants. The 707-hectare park is home to many landmarks, such as the residences of the Irish President and the US ambassador, the Wellington Testimonial, the Papal Cross, and the Victorian People's Flower Gardens. If the native wildlife isn't putting on a show, Dublin Zoo, located inside the entrance, is open all year round.

Monday to Sunday, 24 hours.

—

Parkgate Street, Dublin 7
phoenixpark.ie

St Stephen's Green

If you've been shopping on nearby Grafton Street, you can rest your weary bones in this beautiful city-centre park, depending on the weather, of course. Its 9 hectares are neat and well looked after, with flowers beds, a playground, a lake, and a fountain, and it's where lots of species of birds call home. In sunnier spells this park is packed to capacity with students and suited office workers eating lunch *al fresco*.

Monday to Saturday, 7.30am to dusk; Sunday, 9.30am to dusk.

—

St Stephen's Green Square, Dublin 2
ststephensgreenpark.ie

Check What's On

The Abbey Theatre
The Button Factory
Irish Film Institute
The Sugar Club
Vicar Street
Whelan's

The
Abbey
Theatre

First opened in 1904 by writer W.B. Yeats and dramatist and folklorist Lady Gregory, the Abbey Theatre has nurtured many of Ireland's leading playwrights for over a century. Today, its mission statement remains the same: 'To bring upon the stage the deeper emotions of Ireland,' and it does so by staging the work of many noted Irish playwrights, living and dead. While the theatre is strongly rooted in traditional Irish culture, it doesn't shy away from the experimental, particularly when it comes to programming and staging.

—

26-27 Lower Abbey Street, Dublin 1
abbeytheatre.ie
+353 1 878 7222

The Button Factory

The Button Factory is an intimate live music venue in Temple Bar. The building in which it resides stands on Curved Street; when approaching from the main Temple Bar Square you'll see the iconic Wall of Fame that celebrates Ireland's rock legends, then an abstract portrait of author and musician B.P. Fallon by Irish contemporary artist Maser, that gazes down approvingly on the venue's main door. Inside, there is a big dance floor and a seated balcony, with a combined capacity of 650 people. Check the website for current listings for club nights, and gigs by up-and-coming local and international acts.

—

Curved Street, Temple Bar, Dublin 2
buttonfactory.ie
+353 1 670 9202

Irish Film Institute

Tucked away in Temple Bar, the entrance to the IFI is modest, but its inner atrium is a bright and airy haven for cinema lovers. The IFI is Ireland's cultural institution for film, and alongside its valuable work in preserving and promoting Irish cinema, it specialises in screening those films you won't find in the multiplex. A weekly programme, dense with documentaries, indies and foreign films, is interspersed with special screenings, talks and events. As well as three accessible screens, there is a shop specialising in Irish film writing and international DVDs, and a café bar that is popular with casual diners as well as cinemagoers.

—

6 Eustace Street, Dublin 2
ifi.ie
+353 1 679 3477

The Sugar Club

This live-music venue and nightclub was once the home of the Irish Film Theatre, and it has preserved the tiered layout of the main space. It has been updated to include plush seats and tables, a cocktail bar, a high-end sound system and a state-of-the art digital projector. Check out their website to see what's on, as the Sugar Club prides itself on its diverse programme of events. The combination of stylish, unique elements, a cool crowd, and great music is the perfect formula for a good night out.

—

8 Lower Leeson Street, Dublin 2
thesugarclub.com
+353 1 678 7188

Vicar Street

Ask a Dubliner their favourite place to see a gig and chances are their response will be Vicar Street. With a maximum capacity of 1,500 people, good views are all but guaranteed, but despite its relatively small size it has an excellent reputation for drawing significant international acts (including Bob Dylan and Neil Young). The venue has been a frequent and deserving recipient of the Irish Music Venue of the Year award; however its clever layout also makes it the ideal venue for stand-up comedy. Arrive in time to grab a drink in the bar, which is, like the theatre space itself, simultaneously open and intimate.

—

58-59 Thomas Street, Dublin 2
vicarstreet.com
+353 1 775 5800

Whelan's

Whelan's has been a cornerstone of Dublin's music scene for over twenty-five years. With live music seven nights a week, it made its name with performances by the likes of Jeff Buckley and Nick Cave, and nowadays you'll find top alternative acts like Father John Misty or Dan Deacon on the bill. Have a pint in the front pub in the early evening, while the sun still brightens the wood-heavy interiors, and watch as the diverse crowds steadily arrive and the venue unfolds. In all, there are three rooms that offer a wide variety of music, mostly hovering in and around the indie scene, alongside the odd comedy gig or silent disco. A dependable location for entertainment and convivial crowds every night of the week.

—

25 Wexford Street, Dublin 2
whelanslive.com
+353 1 478 0766

Before you visit Dublin, you might want to check out these books and films to give you a better sense of the city.

Books

At Swim-Two-Birds
Flann O'Brien

Flann O'Brien is the pen name of Brian O'Nolan, who also wrote political satire under the name Myles na gCopaleen. The much-loved *At Swim-Two-Birds* is a complex and hilarious work of metafiction, in which an unnamed student relays three initially unrelated tales in the most convoluted manner, interweaving Irish mythology with anecdotes of drunken debauchery on the streets of Dublin. Like many literary masterpieces, it was initially met with a lukewarm response from the critics, but became a beloved novel of many of the significant writers of the time, notably James Joyce and Anthony Burgess.

Dubliners
James Joyce

Dubliners is James Joyce at his most accessible, which is not to say that the fifteen stories within are lacking in complexity or darkness. The language is simple but extremely detailed, creating realistic scenarios and evocative Dublin scenes. As the book progresses, the protagonist in each story is older, beginning with a young boy's experience of death in 'The Sisters' and culminating in the most famous story, 'The Dead', a lengthy rumination on life and death that was adapted for the screen by John Huston in 1987. *Dubliners* is an excellent introduction to Joyce's daunting body of work, and required reading for an insight into Dublin at a time of colossal change.

The Gathering
Anne Enright

On the face of it, a well-trodden plot about a family gathering in their home town for a wake, 2007 Man Booker prize-winning *The Gathering* departs from the usual clichés due to the stark lyricism of Anne Enright's storytelling. As Veronica Hegarty mourns her beloved brother Liam, and prepares to assemble along with her mother and remaining siblings in Dublin, she is dogged by a blurry but possibly traumatic memory involving Liam as a child in their grandmother's house. As Veronica comes to terms with Liam's life and death, Enright deftly constructs an Irish family history where 'joy and woe are woven fine'.

The Snapper
Roddy Doyle

The second novel in Doyle's Barrytown Trilogy, following the working-class Rabbitte family, *The Snapper* is the story of twenty-year-old Sharon, who finds herself unexpectedly pregnant after being taken advantage of by an older man, and the impact that the ensuing attention and speculation has on her and her family. Mostly written in dialogue, which is rich with Dublin dialect, it is an extremely funny and warm look at the family dynamic, particularly between father and daughter. Adapted into a film in 1993, the story has a big place in the city's heart; in 2015 a plaque was unveiled at the Rotunda Hospital on Parnell Square, where Sharon's fictional baby was born.

Films

Adam & Paul
(2004)

While it is certainly not the most heart-warming of films, this tale of two young Dublin heroin addicts provides an insight into the real and ever-growing problems of drug addiction and homelessness in Dublin. Directed by Lenny Abrahamson, who brought us other gems such as *Room* and *What Richard Did*, the screenplay was written by Mark O'Halloran, who plays Adam in the film. It is a bleak, funny and moving depiction of the reality of drug abuse and provides a perspective of Dublin that you won't find in the travel guides.

The Commitments
(1991)

Set against the gritty backdrop of the pre-Celtic Tiger northside of Dublin, *The Commitments* is the story of Jimmy Rabbitte, an aspiring Brian Epstein who gathers a group of his working-class friends to form an unlikely soul band. Based on a book by Roddy Doyle, it is a riotously funny film full of filthy language and brilliant music. The cast, most of whom had never acted before, were chosen for their musical ability, and many have since enjoyed successful music careers, including Bronagh Gallagher, Maria Doyle Kennedy, and Glen Hansard, defying the expectations foisted upon their on-screen counterparts: 'Is this the band then? Betcha U2 are shittin' themselves.'

Michael Collins
(1996)

This Neil Jordan classic relates the last days of Michael Collins, a 1916 revolutionary. After the uprising he went on to negotiate the Anglo-Irish Treaty which gave Ireland the status of a 'Free State' and established the border with Northern Ireland. This treaty subsequently led to

the Irish Civil War, in which Collins was assassinated. The Civil War is still a contentious issue, particularly among the older generation in Ireland, and as expected, the glorification of Michael Collins was not to everyone's liking. Starring Liam Neeson and Julia Roberts, it's a great film to provide you with a bit of background to this tumultuous period of Irish history, evidence of which you will encounter many times during your visit.

Once
(2007)

Once is the story of a vacuum repair-man (Glen Hansard) and an immigrant flower seller (Markéta Irglová) who both harbour musical ambitions, and their blossoming friendship over one week in Dublin. Made for an extremely low budget over seventeen days in the city, the film became a massive sleeper hit. It was critically acclaimed, championed by Hollywood A-listers, and went on to win the Academy Award for Best Original Song for 'Falling Slowly'. An adaptation for the stage has been a hit on both side of the Atlantic, but the film's low-fi romance is enriched by its naturalistic Dublin backdrop.

Check out these sites and accounts for the most up-do-date events and insights into Dublin life:

Influencers

Totally Dublin
totallydublin.ie

For the latest news and events in Dublin.

entertainment.ie
entertainment.ie

Up-to-date cinema, music and event listings and reviews.

LeCool Dublin
dublin.lecool.com

Unmissable cultural events and leisure activities.

No More Workhorse
nomoreworkhorse.com

Arts site covering events and all aspects of culture, allowing you to 'appear highbrow without trying'.

DublinTown
dublintown.ie

A guide for locals and visitors alike, operated by local creative talent and business owners.

HeadStuff
headstuff.org

High-quality content with articles, events and podcasts to broaden the mind.

Lovin' Dublin
lovindublin.com

The latest food, lifestyle and culture news in Dublin.

Nialler 9
nialler9.com

DJ, gig curator and music blogger, Niall Byrne is

Dublin's leading authority on music.

French Foodie in Dublin
frenchfoodieindublin.com

The best in Dublin dining; also operates deliciousdublintours.com, providing culinary walking tours.

Ireland on Twitter
@ireland

Curated by a new person every week, @ireland gives unique perspectives on life around the country.

Tips from the inside: we asked some top Dublin creatives for their favourite spots

Contributors

Andrea Horan
@andreahoran

Andrea Horan is the owner of the colourful and joyous nail salon Tropical Popical (tropicalpopical.com). She is also a prominent social campaigner.

'My favourite restaurant In Dublin is Coppinger Row (pg. 57). I'm only delighted that Charlotte Quay (charlottequay.ie) has opened too so I have some variety of how I give the Bereen brothers all my wages! I love the vibes in Coppinger, because as I get older, I don't want to go to clubs so Coppinger has the feeling of going out for craic with the added bonus of delish cocktails and food.

'If I get a huge spark of energy on a Saturday night, I love Mother (pg. 101). I love fun music – I don't take it seriously at all so Mother is great for disco and fun.

'L'Gueuleton (lgueuleton.com, 1 Fade St, Dublin 2) needs to get a mention, for their steak alone. But also for their new after-dinner drinks and dancing that they've started at the weekends.'

Bob Johnston
@gutterbookshop

Bob Johnston is an independent bookseller and owner of the Gutter Bookshop (pg. 30).

'Dublin is getting better for vegan eating choices but the current reigning queen of vegan eating is Sova Vegan Butcher at 51 Pleasants Street, Dublin 2, who combine innovative cooking with great tasting plates of food and very friendly staff. A treat of an evening out that's not just for vegans!

'PantiBar on Capel Street (pg. 104) is a gay bar that welcomes everyone. From a chilled after-work pint to full-on drag shows hosted by international superstar Panti Bliss, it's a friendly neighbourhood bar that is fast becoming a Dublin institution.

'The RHA (Royal Hibernian Academy) at 15 Ely Place is an often overlooked gallery space for contemporary Irish art that never fails to offer something interesting and stimulating to look at. And if you get your act together you can get tickets for their occasional Hennessy Lost Fridays series, which mixes art with top DJs and exquisite cocktails for a slightly different start to the weekend. I also love the stunning octagonal Exhibition Room in the City Assembly House on South William Street, the first purpose-built public art gallery in either Britain or Ireland, which is slowly being restored but retains a faded grandeur.'

Sonya Lennon
@sonyalennon

Sonya Lennon is a designer and tech entreprenuer who, with her business partner Brendan Courtney, established the label Lennon Courtney.

'I have a love affair with Forest & Marcy (forestandmarcy.ie, 126 Leeson Street Upper, Dublin 4) the spin-off restaurant of the fabulous Forest Avenue (pg. 62). A wonderful room full of interesting people with stunning food to share. The theme is forward-thinking foraging, utterly modern but grounded into the land.

'I'm not a fan of shiny, glam and sanitised when it comes to bars. I'd much rather take my chances in the crazy world of the Hacienda (pg. 89) in the heart of the historical Smithfield Market. It's down and dirty and an utter melting pot of humanity. Expect to be vetted at the door, but not in a bad way, to partake in late-night drinking and pool.

'My favourite place in Dublin is the South Wall, a Victorian masterpiece of engineering that strides a mile into Dublin Port. Like all good things, it's a pilgrimage to get there but definitely worth the trek.'

Fatti Burke
@fattiburke

Kathi 'Fatti' Burke is a successful artist and illustrator, and co-creator of the award-winning books *Irelandopedia* and *Historopedia*.

'You might come to The Square Ball (the-square-ball.com, 45 Hogan Pl, Grand Canal Dock, Dublin 2) for the great selection of beers and cocktails – the rotating taps showcasing seasonal beers is always fun for tasting new brews – but you'll definitely stay for the games. The Square Ball has recently amassed over 500 board games, basically any one you can think of, which you can play in the pub for a small fee. That, plus their weekly table quizzes, bingo, match screenings and the unreal BBQ grub in their Fowl Play kitchen makes for a guaranteed good night out.

'Based in an impressive Georgian townhouse off Stephen's Green, the Little Museum of Dublin (littlemuseum.ie, 15 St Stephen's Green, Dublin 2) is home to a collection of curiosities stretching from floor to ceiling – every wall is covered with nostalgic tidbits and beautiful relics dating from across the last two centuries. The overwhelming hoard of artefacts is accompanied by a tour, which is where you can really start to appreciate the importance of the little treasures surrounding you.

'I love Galliot et Grey (59 Clanbrassil Street Lower, Dublin 2). French-style pizzas, cooked in a wood-fired oven, topped with Emmental cheese and fresh ingredients. Just one of the best places to meet friends and have an insanely good pizza (my favourite is the Four Cheese, but honestly they're all fantastic). You can even grab a beer from the Headline Bar and have it at your table, cause they're sound like that.'

Annie Atkins
@AnnieAtkins

Annie Atkins is an award-winning graphic designer for film, whose work on *The Grand Budapest Hotel* brought her international acclaim. A regular lecturer in her field, she also runs weekend workshops in Dublin.

'The Phoenix Park (pg. 120) is mostly woodland, tall grass, and vast green expanse – over 1,500 acres of it. I like walking here on summer evenings, looking out for bats. Watch out for the herds of deer, too.

'Sweny's Chemist (sweny.ie, 1 Lincoln Place, Dublin 2) is where Leopold Bloom bought his bar of lemon soap in Ulysses. You can still buy soap here, but it's now also home to poetry readings, books, and memorabilia from James Joyce's Dublin.'

Rosaleen McMeel
@rosiemcmeel

Rosaleen McMeel is Editor of *IMAGE* magazine, one of Ireland's leading fashion publications.

'Inspired by the Italian restaurants of 1950's America, Luna on Drury Street (p.65) instantly transports me to another time. The menu is sumptuous and the service, headed up by manager Declan Maxwell (formerly of Chapter One) is consistently superb. Plus, the waiters wear red velvet jackets designed by Louis Copeland, which adds huge charm and elegance.

'Hang Dai (hangdaichinese.com) on Camden Street is a fun new addition to the city. From the front-of-house staff with buckets of personality to the train carriage interiors and tasty mix of plates, this will be a dining experience you'll never forget.

'When it comes to bars, I prefer a no-frills experience and Dublin offers some of the finest that (made-up) genre has to offer. While O'Donoghues on Merrion Row (p.94) will forever remain a firm favourite, Bruxelles (bruxelles.ie), just off Grafton Street, can't be beaten for late-night dancing (read: swaying to the beat). Prepare to have beer spilled on your feet and to make friends within five minutes of your arrival.

'For shopping, Brown Thomas (p.27) will always hold a special place in my heart due to its international collections and first class service, but it's the smaller boutiques that really offer something unique to visitors. Loulerie (loulerie.com) on Chatham Row, run by Louise Stokes, is a small independent jewellery store stocking both her own designs, and high-fashion jewellery by international brands such as Oscar De La Renta and Alexis Bittar.

'It might seem a cliché, but the Guinness Storehouse (p. 40) is genuinely one of my favourite places to take visitors. You'll not only discover what goes into the making of this black brew but if you're planning on tasting your first pint, where better than in the 360°Gravity Bar overlooking the entire city?'

Photography Credits

Pg. 6 Conor Clinch, Pg.8 Getty Images/David Soanes Photography, Pg.13 Getty Images/Paul M O'Connell, Pg.14 Number 31, Pg.16 The Dean, Leo Byrne, Pg.17 The Generator, Nerissa Sparkman, Pg.18 Kelly's Hotel, Pg.19 Getty Images/Lonely Planet Images, Pg.20 The Merrion, Pg.21 Number 31, Pg.22 The Shelbourne, Pg.23 The Shelbourne, David Cantwell, Pg.24 Article, Pg.26 Article, Pg.27 Brown Thomas, Pg.28 Fallon & Byrne, Siobhan Byrne, Pg.29 Folkster, Pg.30 The Gutter Bookshop, Pg.31 Hodges Figgis, Gareth Byrne, Pg.32 Indigo & Cloth, Pg.33 Indigo & Cloth, Pg.34 Industry, Pg.35 Nowhere, Pg.36 Parfumarija, Pg.37 Parfumarija, Pg.38 Mark Colliton, Pg.40 Guinness, Enda Cavanagh, Pg.41 Guinness, Enda Cavanagh, Pg.42 IMMA, Kunst Halle Sankt Gallen,, St.Gallen, 2012. Courtesy the artist. Photo, Gunnar Meier, Pg.43 IMMA, Pg.44 Kilmainham Gaol, Pg.46 National Gallery, Roy Hewson, Pg.47 Anton_ Ivanov/Shutterstock.com, Pg.48 Natural History Museum, Pg.49 Getty Images/Exotica.im, Pg.50 Mark Colliton, Pg.52 Brother Hubbard, Pg.54 777, Pg.55 Bastible, Pg.56 Bunsen, Pg.57 Coppinger Row, Terry McDonagh, Pg.58 Cotto, Pg.59 Delanhunt, Pg.60 Etto, Paolo Polesel, Pg.61 Fade Street Social, Damian Bligh, Pg.62 Forest Avenue, Pg.63 Forest Avenue, Pg.64 Klaw, Pg.65 Luna, Ste Murray, Pg.66 Patrick.Wong/Shutterstock.com, Pg.67 Patrick Guilbaud, Barry McCall, Pg.68 Pickle, David Conn, Pg.69 Skinflint, Pg.70 Taste at Rustic, Damian Bligh, Pg.71 The Vintage Kitchen, Pg.72 The Winding Stair, Pg.73 The Winding Stair, Pg.74 Wuff, Taine King, Pg.75 Wuff, Taine King, Pg.76 The Fumbally, Shantanu Starick, Pg.78 3FE, Pg.79 Clement & Pekoe, Pg.80 The Fumbally, Pg.81 The Fumbally, Shantanu Starick, Pg.82 Kaph, Pg.83 Two Boys Brew, Pg.84 Brother Hubbard, Pg.85 Brother Hubbard, Pg.86 Getty Images/ David Toase, Pg.88 Getty Images/Lonely Planet, Pg.89 The Hacienda, Azzy O'Connor, Pg.90 Kehoe's, Tyler W. Stipp/Shutterstock.co, Pg.91 L. Mulligan Grocer, Pg.92 The Long Hall, Mary Wright, Pg.93 Getty Images/Tim Clayton/Contributor, Pg.94 Getty Images/Tim Clayton/Con-tributor, Pg.95 Getty Images/Robert Alexander/Contributor, Pg.96 The Liquor Rooms, Aidan Oliver Weldon, Pg.98 Chris Cooper-Smith/Alamy Stock Photo, Pg.99 The Chelsea Drugstore, Pg.100 The Dice Bar, Pg.101 Mother, Pg.102 No Name Bar, Peter Love, Pg.103 P. Macs, Pg.104 PantiBar, Pg.105 Pygmalion, Azzy O'Connor, Pg.106 The Liquor Rooms, Pg.107 The Liquor Rooms, Aidan Oliver Weldon, Pg.108 The Workman's Club, Pg.109 The Workman's Club, Pg.110 Anna Levan/Shutterstock.com, Pg.112 Ha'penny Flea, tbc, Pg.114 Brendan Donnelly/Ala-my Stock Photo, Pg.115 Semmick Photo/Shutterstock.com, Pg.116 Getty Images/David Soanes Photography, Pg.118 Getty Images/David Soanes Photography, Pg.119 Getty Images/David Soanes Photography, Pg.121 St Stephen's Green, Niall O'Donovan, Pg.122 The Abbey Theatre,

Ros Kavanagh, Pg.124 The Abbey Theatre, Ros Kavanagh, Pg.126 The Button Factory, William Murphy, Pg.127 IFI, Pg.128 The Sugar Club, Sean Smyth, Pg.129 Vicar Street, Pg.130 Whelan's, Pg.131 Whelan's, Dara Munnis, Pg.132 David Soanes/Shutterstock.com